STORIE DEL MO

DANIELA CAVINI

Behind the Medici Men: the Ladies

MAURO PAGLIAI EDITORE

Originally published as: *Le Magnifiche dei Medici. Dodici ritratti*
Mauro Pagliai, Florence, October 2017
1st reprint: February 2018
2nd reprint: July 2019

1st English edition: April 2018 (translation: Aelmuire Helen Cleary)
1st reprint: July 2023

www.mauropagliai.it

© 2023 LEONARDO LIBRI srl
Via Livorno, 8/32 - 50142 Firenze - Tel. 055 73787
info@leonardolibri.com - www.leonardolibri.com

ISBN 978-88-564-0383-1

Summary

PREFACE

In Tuscany, if someone says Lorenzo you immediately think of the most famous and cultured of the Medici (and the first line of his most famous poem "How fair is youth…"). They say Cosimo, and the figure that springs to mind is bound to be the most powerful and valiant of the Medici (and Vasari's commissioner to boot). Then there's Giuliano: the most unlucky of the Medici (thanks to the bloodthirsty and rightly-named 'crazy' Pazzi clan). And the last Grand Duke of the dynasty, Gian Gastone: he was a Medici too. The most reviled, depraved and decadent of the lot, but famous all the same: born a Medici and a Medici he remained. But what about the ladies of the house? The distaff side of the dynasty that made Florence the great city that went down in history? Who remembers them, apart from the scholars and the aficionados of Medici Tuscany? Maybe if someone says Lucrezia you might think of Borgia, or if they say Isabella, perhaps you would associate it with Rossellini. But if they were to say Alfonsina, you probably wouldn't be able to think of anyone with that name.

However, joking apart, this is serious matter. In history books women have almost always been relegated to the wings, behind or next to the men, even though they were frequently responsible for the men's choices, merits or mistakes. And the House of Medici is no exception to the rule. Lucrezia, a poetess who was possibly shrewder in business than in her versifying, was the energetic wife of Piero il Gottoso and the mother of Lorenzo il Magnifico, on whom she imposed the unpopular Clarice Orsini as a bride to further the political interests of the family. Then Eleonora of Toledo, the beloved wife of Cosimo I, who was also an expert manager of both their private property and the state finances. She was the first woman to set foot in the Palazzo della Signoria to share in the management of power. And then there were two Queens of France, Maria and Caterina. Last of all, the unfortunate Anna Maria Luisa, left alone and childless, who after the death of her brother Gian Gastone was forced to hand over the throne of Tuscany to the House of Lorraine. That is, to the Holy Roman Emperor. But not before she had put pen to paper to establish that all the assets – palaces, works of art, books and collections – were to remain in Florence "for the ornament of the State, for the use of the Public and to attract the curiosity of Foreigners." This was in 1737, and if we can now visit the Uffizi with all its treasures, it is thanks to her. And yet how many people, even Florentines, know this? Matteo Renzi tried to make amends of a sort when, as President of the Provincial Authority, he made her one of the symbols of 'Florentine Genius'. Nevertheless, Anna Maria Luisa de' Medici, Electress Palatine, after whom the Lungarno running beneath the Uffizi Gallery is named, is not particularly popular even here in her home town.

And so we have these Medici women: feisty or demure, cynical or lovable, bold or ingenuous, and all neglected. Consequently, to mark the year of the Medici and the Italian TV series that recounted (and embroidered) their adventures, here at the *Corriere Fiorentino* we felt the time was ripe to dust the cobwebs off these ladies. And what better choice to write this book than Daniela Cavini: a meticulous and curious journalist with a pleasant style, and a Florentine in love with her city. The result is a series of twelve portraits, one finer than the next. A small contribution to memory offered to those with a passion for history, and another piece in the wonderful jigsaw of Florence. It's a brand the Florentines are proud of; they take pride in their past. Who knows what Florence would have been now if it hadn't been for the men of the House of Medici? And the women.

Paolo Ermini

INTRODUCTION

These are (extra)ordinary women. Not all of them possessed special qualities, quite the opposite, but from a tender age most had to address exacting trials that forged their temperaments and moulded their characters. This transformed them from ordinary noble housewives, devoted to bearing and rearing children, into veritable leaders.

Entering the ranks of the most illustrious Italian dynasty by birth or by marriage, they lived as consorts, constrained to make their way in a world designed and governed by men. Even when it was they who guided the family, their importance was not acknowledged. Their dowries included surnames exploited for social climbing by the merchants turned bankers, later raised to dukes. And there they were, thriftily running the household, putting up with infidelity, bearing legitimate children, ennobling the dynasty, managing the finances and sometimes even directing the political fortunes of the lineage. These women were willing to sacrifice everything for that surname, worn like a yoke but with impeccable grace. And when required they were equally willing to take a back seat, as if it were the most natural thing in the world.

At best, the river of history flows silently over the Medici women. Hardly anyone speaks of Maria Salviati, who fashioned the genius of Cosimo I. All that anyone knows about Isabella de' Medici is that she came to a sticky end, despite the fact that she was the last true heir to the spirit of the Magnifico. When history does bother itself with the ladies it is because they are judged Machiavellian, diabolical or wicked. For example, Caterina the bloody Queen of France. Or Alfonsina Orsini, "an ambitious and importunate female," as adulated in life as she was vilified in death. Had they been men they would have been considered able and enterprising, but as women they were seen as perverse and pernicious. Or dismissed as fools, like the other French queen, Maria, denied any tribute whatsoever from posterity. But what do we really know about these indomitable and often unhappy brides, bent to the will of a history lived and told by men? Sometimes we don't even know when they were born.

The short portraits that follow certainly don't aspire to add anything new to the great fresco of Medici achievements. Rather they attempt to bring out a flicker of the soul, the concealed impulse of a decision, the shadowy reason behind grief or error. These are private sketches which clearly do not absolve all guilt but do at least seek to discern into which pool of melancholy – of the kind all women succumb to at some point in their lives – the Medici women fell, and when and how they emerged from it, if they ever did.

But what these stories also indicate is that, at crucial moments of Medici history, it was indeed the women who took the helm and got the dynasty back on its feet. Lucrezia, for example, who took the reins when her husband Piero was ill, passing on the family fortune intact to her son Lorenzo (who then made short work of spending it). Or Alfonsina, who brought the dynasty back to Florence after it had been driven out in 1494. Eleonora, a consummate manager, who lent her husband huge sums of money, swelling the family coffers. Right through to the master stroke of the last of the Medici: the 'Family Pact' drawn up between Anna Maria Luisa and the new foreign sovereigns, which ensured that none of the treasures of the dynasty could be "transferred out of the capital and the State". This anomalous and ingenious contract placed the family heritage in the hands of the city, redeeming the folly of the last generations to rule the Duchy and guaranteeing a future for Florence.

Naturally, all these portraits build on what has previously been written by Piero Bargellini, Pina Marzi Ciotti, Arnaldo D'Addario, Umberto Dorini, Anna Maria Francini Ciaranfi, Emma Micheletti, Carlo Pellegrini, G.F. Young and Marcello Vannucci. These stories would never have been possible without the *Corriere Fiorentino*, the editor-in-chief Paolo Ermini and Lorella Romagnoli, senior editor for culture, to whom I express my gratitude.

Daniela Cavini

LE DONNE DEI MEDICI

Giovanni di Bicci
(1360-1429)
(Piccarda Bueri)

Cosimo Il Vecchio
(1389-1464)
(Contessina Bardi)

Piero il Gottoso
(1416-1469)
**(Lucrezia
Tornabuoni)**

Giovanni
(1421-1466)

Carlo
(naturale)

Lorenzo il Magnifico
(1449-1492)
(Clarice Orsini)

Giuliano
1453-1478

Giulio
(1478-1534)
(Papa Clemente VII)

Piero II
(1471-1503)
(Alfonsina Orsini)

Giovanni
(1475-1521)
(Papa Leone X)

Giuliano
Duca di Nemours
(1479-1516)
(Philiberte de Savoie)

Ippolito
Cardinale
(naturale)
(1511-1535)

Lorenzo II
Duca d'Urbino
(1492-1519)
**(Madeleine de la Tour
d'Auvergne)**

Caterina
(1519-1589)
**(Regina di Francia,
Enrico II)**

Alessandro
(naturale)
(1510-1537)
Primo duca di Firenze

Lorenzo
(1395-1440)
(**Ginevra Cavalcanti**)

Pier Francesco
(1430-1477)

Lorenzo
(1463-1503)

Giovanni
(1467-1498)
(**Caterina Sforza**)

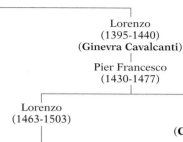

Pier Francesco
(1487-1525)

Giovanni dalle Bande Nere
(1498-1526)
(**Maria Salviati**)

Lorenzino
(1514-1547)

Cosimo I
granduca
(1519-1574)
(**Eleonora di Toledo**)

Francesco I
(1541-1587)
(1. **Giovanna d'Austria**
2. **Bianca Cappello**)

Ferdinando I
(1549-1609)
(**Cristina di Lorena**)

Isabella

Maria
(1573-1642)
(Regina di Francia
Enrico IV)

Cosimo II
(1590-1621)
(**Maria Maddalena d'Austria**)

Ferdinando II
(1610-1670)
(**Vittoria della Rovere**)

Cosimo III
(1642-1723)
(**Margherita d'Orléans**)

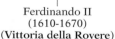

Anna Maria Luisa
(1667-1743)
(Elettore Palatino)

Gian Gastone
(1671-1737)
(**Anna Maria Francesca di Sassonia**)

LUCREZIA, THE MAN OF THE FAMILY

In 1443 Lucrezia Tornabuoni was given in marriage to Piero dei Medici, the eldest son of Cosimo il Vecchio, head of the most important international bank of the time.

Lucrezia was no beauty and did not pass on good looks to her son Lorenzo either, although he was dubbed 'the Magnificent' for other reasons. She had a dull complexion, was short-sighted and also suffered from aphonia. Ghirlandaio's portrait in the National Gallery in London shows her with a long nose and protruding chin. "*Vetusta, non pulcra*" as the intellectuals of the time put it. However, Lucrezia was intelligent and cultured and she was of aristocratic birth. This prestigious match marked a large step up in the social ascent of the family of merchants turned bankers. The Tornaquinci, who then became the Torna-Buoni, were indeed of noble origins. They had settled in Florence in the tenth century, had fought against Barbarossa and were Guelphs to the core.

Lucrezia Tornabuoni

Birth of Saint John the Baptist,
detail showing Lucrezia Tornabuoni (second from right).
Domenico Ghirlandaio, Santa Maria Novella, Florence

They were part of the city oligarchy of feudal origin, the 'magnates' who always headed the institutions of the commune. When she entered the house of Medici, Lucrezia brought with her a meagre dowry, only 1,000 florins, but her marriage with Piero sealed an alliance with a dynasty of ancient lineage, which had also helped to save Cosimo just a few years earlier.

A plot had been hatched in 1433 by a handful of noble families led by Rinaldo degli Albizi. They wanted to get rid of the Medici, resenting their boundless wealth, growing prestige and influence over the people. Cosimo was imprisoned in Arnolfo's tower in Palazzo Vecchio, where he managed to avoid being poisoned only because he succeeded in having his food brought from home. Then he was exiled to Venice. However, the *pater patriae* was a political genius and adept at exploiting the persuasive power of money. Distributing largesse without request for return – an astute policy in a city athirst for money – the old lion managed to turn the situation around, regaining the favour of the populace. Now the time had come to repay those who had supported him, and the Tornabuoni marriage ratified the pact. Lucrezia's brother Giovanni joined the family bank, and the young Lucrezia herself was welcomed as a precious link in a pow-

The elderly Cosimo de' Medici (on the left)
riding next to his son Piero, on the right.
Benozzo Gozzoli, Cappella dei Magi, Palazzo Medici Riccardi, Firenze

17

er system of broad intentions. With her, Cosimo had come up trumps and it didn't take him long to realise it.

Among the tasks assigned to Lucrezia by her husband Piero, who was sound of mind but ailing of body, was that of distributing alms to the needy. But, as well as having a literary education, the noblewoman also knew her business, which she managed along with her lands and income, handling money with the ease learnt from her ancestors. She realised that to help the people it was crucial to fuel the support network and she rapidly set about it. She financed craftsmen and merchants and gave generously to churches and convents. She revealed her strategy in a letter: "What is good for Florence and Tuscany is also good for the Medici family."

Lucrezia was firm and she had a nose for business. She was so good at winning people over that her father-in-law Cosimo declared her to be "the only man in the family." The people of Florence felt more or less the same, calling her 'the haven of all mysteries.' Especially after Cosimo's death it was she who kept the show on the road, shrewdly managing the household goods, as well as maintaining the relations which her husband Piero, by then bedridden by gout, was unable to manage. And she did it all with the utmost discretion, always one step behind. She had learnt from her father-in-law.

To the outside world Lucrezia – a poet and intellectual, patron of Poliziano and Pulci – was an affectionate mother devoted to her children. After accepting Piero's illegitimate daughter Maria (an inconvenience not uncommon at the time) Lucrezia gave birth to two girls, Bianca and Nannina, and two boys, Lorenzo and Giuliano. She wanted the best possible education for her children, giving them over to the

This is widely believed to be a portrait of the young Lorenzo il Magnifico, painted by Benozzo Gozzoli in the Chapel of the Magi, Palazzo Medici-Riccardi, Florence

humanist eclecticism of Marsilio Ficino and the study of Socrates and Alcibiades. She taught the Latin herself, writing to her husband from the residence at Cafaggiolo that they were progressing with Ovid, and that Giuliano had four books on the go, from history to fables. It was his mother that transmitted to Lorenzo an education pivoting on antiquity, on Plato's Philosopher Kings, which was to make him the Magnifico of Florence. Their relationship was very close: it was she who reared him like a prince, "brought up to seduce" (Tim Parks). When the time came to choose a bride for him, Lucrezia's intuition hit the mark. Cosimo had taken a Bardi, Piero a Tornabuoni; for Lorenzo, his mother looked further afield, beyond Florence, to open up more ambitious horizons. With Lucrezia – the only man in the family – the policy of matrimonial alliances made the quality leap essential for the rise of the dynasty: the link with the Papacy. The choice fell on a member of the Roman Orsini family and, good merchant that she was, Lucrezia herself went to Rome to inspect the goods. From there she wrote to her husband, reporting that the girl's bosom appeared to be "of good quality", even though the Roman fashion imposed gowns that were too high-necked to be able to see it. The deal was struck. Lorenzo married Clarice, to the veiled discontent of the Florentines who, according to Machiavelli, believed that "he who does not want citizens as relatives wants them as slaves."

It was not to be a happy marriage. Lorenzo was never in love with Clarice and ran after other women. But his mother was the only one who was always at his side, especially after Piero's death in 1469, when at the age of twenty Lorenzo found himself the head of the family (and in charge of the city). In the backlash that followed the Pazzi Conspiracy, Lucrezia stood staunchly by her son, supporting him even in his bloody vendetta. When she died, in 1482, the Magnifico wrote to Eleonora d'Este: "I continue to be so disconsolate. I have lost not only my mother but the sole refuge from my many troubles and repose from my many labours." It was (also) due to Lucrezia's stringent management that the conspicuous family fortune passed more or less intact into the hands of the new Lord of Florence. Lorenzo himself was prepared to do anything, except to busy himself with the family bank which in fact rapidly declined.

Clarice, the rose in the shade

Clarice Orsini lived in the shadows. She brought nine children into the world and died young. A 'prickly rose', she tried her best to be a good wife to Lorenzo dei Medici, who did not love her and even during her pregnancies continued to write love sonnets to Lucrezia Donati. However, he did respect her, and no mistress ever took the place of his consort.

Clarice Orsini

The Florentines didn't love her either, just as later they failed to warm to other 'foreign' brides who arrived to snap up the most eligible bachelors in the city. But Clarice knew her place; she was a sensible woman, extremely religious and of irreproachable morality. She wasn't brilliant, but that was not the reason she had been imported from Rome. She was required to supply descendants to the dynasty of Cosimo, the *pater patriae*,

Lorenzo il Magnifico

to bear children to the rising star of Lorenzo. And that is what she did. Even more importantly, the Roman bride represented a crucial step forward in the ambitions of the family, which through her was able to forge bonds far from the banks of the Arno, paving the way for two future Medici Popes.

On 4 June 1469 Florence celebrated the marriage of Piero's heir, destined to succeed his father in a matter of months. Over three days of feasting the Florentines consumed 150 calves, 4,000 capons and almost 2 tons of sweetmeats. Lorenzo and Clarice didn't even know each other. The young lady had been pulled out of a hat by Lorenzo's mother, Lucrezia Tornabuoni, who had gone to Rome in person to finalise the choice. "The girl seems to me quite tall, pretty and fair-skinned," she wrote to her husband detained in Florence by illness. We know hardly anything about this girl "who did not walk haughtily", not even her date of birth. Lorenzo submitted without making a fuss: "I, Lorenzo, took as my wife Clarice, the daughter of Jacobo Orsini, or rather she was given to me." The scion of the Medici lineage was not required to have any great dealings with his young wife, who remained intimately extraneous to his spirit and his interests, and to the role of mistress of the most culturally fertile house of the Italian Renaissance.

From the Villa of Cafaggiolo (in the photo) Clarice Orsini sent hares and phea-sants to her husband Lorenzo de Medici, who rarely put in an appearance

Cafaggiolo, Giusto Utens, 1599-1602, Florence

Clarice did not live very much in the residence of Via Larga, which was a hub of Neoplatonic thought and crucible of the arts. In the twenty years she spent with her husband she was almost always confined with her children in the Villa of Cafaggiolo in Mugello where Lorenzo, who was not fond of hunting, rarely put in an appearance. But she went on expecting him, and would send him game for his dinners with Marsilio Ficino and his companions. "I am sending you a pheasant and a hare," she wrote, "because it seems such a shame for us to eat them here among ourselves." Lorenzo remained aloof: he had a city to keep under control, beauty to foster, a bank to be pushed towards a magnificent decline. Clarice insisted: "I would have dearly loved it if you had come to enjoy them here with us, it's three evenings now that we waited for you, up to three hours." But to no avail; the mind of the poet-prince was occupied with other matters. Florence was his personal work of art, and he had problems with the Pope and the rivalry of the Pazzi. Having survived the Conspiracy of 1478, his rapid and brutal revenge strengthened his hold over the city. Then he jumped

Bust of Lorenzo
il Magnifico.
Pietro Torrigiano,
polychrome terracotta,
Florence

straight into the lion's den, heading for Naples, where he diplomatically succeeded in convincing King Ferrante to withdraw from his alliance with the Pope. Florence was saved and Lorenzo was hailed as the Magnifico. It was no great matter that the Medici bank was in ruins and in three years was forced to close its branches in Milan, Avignon, Bruges, London and Venice. Lorenzo had studied to become the Lord of Florence, not to run the family bank. Now

Lucrezia Donati.
Bust by Giovanni Bastianini

there was no longer any great need of money to govern: Lorenzo's personal charisma was sufficient. Meanwhile, at Cafaggiolo, Clarice was still wooing him with game: "I am sending you these two hares, with my love, so that you will remember me with them." Lorenzo continued to write poems to Lucrezia.

Clarice was estranged by the extraordinary intellectual energy of her husband (and of his circle) and had no interest in literature or social life. To fill her days she frequently went to visit her own family in Rome. Unlike her mother-in-law Lucrezia, who was a cultured intellectual and skilled at cultivating relationships, Clarice settled for asking favours for her brothers and interceding for the religious congregations she was attached to. She knew her place and she stayed there, without getting involved or claiming pre-

The tutor Agnolo Poliziano and the sons of
Lorenzo il Magnifico ascending the stairs.
Domenico Ghirlandaio, Sassetti Chapel, Santa Trinita, Florence

rogatives that did not belong to her, and went on bearing
legitimate children. For their education Lorenzo chose
Poliziano and Pulci, who were artists favoured by his mother Lucrezia rather than teachers. Clarice and the tutors
loathed each other and complained in turn to the Magnifico. "As for Giovanni," wrote Poliziano to Lorenzo, "his
mother occupies him in reading the Psalter. Something
which I cannot under any circumstances commend." The
Psalms versus lascivious Latin writers; the duel about the
educational system flared into open conflict and led to the
dismissal of the intellectual poet. Clarice threw Poliziano
out of Cafaggiolo, replacing him with a priest. Lorenzo did

not bat an eyelid, apart from welcoming the fugitive in Via Larga. Clarice had won. Giovanni – the future Pope Leo X – would study the Psalter. Lorenzo too began to court the new Pope, Innocent VIII, in quest of the cardinal's purple for his son and the ecclesiastical incomes that would tow the family out of the financial doldrums.

Then, while the sermons of Savonarola stripped Christianity of all luxury, leading to the bonfires of works of art and other similar vanities, Clarice began to arrange the marriage of her eldest son Piero with his cousin Alfonsina. She was already suffering from a severe lung condition which carried her off shortly afterwards, before her 35th birthday. Lorenzo wasn't around this time either; he was away at the thermal baths and did not even return for the funeral. He then decided to lift the ban on public festivities, which had been in force since the Pazzi Conspiracy, which seems a somewhat strange way of mourning . . .

Writing to her husband Piero about Clarice, Lucrezia had referred that "she is very modest and will soon learn to adapt to our ways." But that didn't happen. As Piero Bargellini wrote, "Clarice did not let herself be domesticated, and the gentle manners of Palazzo Medici remained alien to her. She retained her character as a firm and strict Roman lady." *Vultui suavis, aspera manui* (Lovely to the eye, sharp to the touch) is the inscription on the rear of a medal on which the Magnifico's wife has the symbol of a prickly rose.

A woman in the background for the most awkward of husbands.

Alfonsina, wearing the trousers

An Italian Lady Macbeth? If she'd been a man she would have been considered shrewd and enterprising. But she was a woman, and so she has gone down in history as a ruthless arriviste. Alfonsina Orsini, a Medici by marriage, epitomises better than any other figure of her time all the Renaissance misogyny towards ladies with aspirations to government.

Alfonsina Orsini

"Neither beautiful nor ugly," Alfonsina entered the Medici ranks in 1487 as the wife of Lorenzo il Magnifico's eldest son, Piero. The marriage broker was her cousin, later mother-in-law, Lorenzo's wife Clarice Orsini. As long as her parents-in-law were alive Alfonsina behaved like any other noblewoman in the family, dedicating herself to procreation. Clarice and Lorenzo were born, named after their grandparents. Meanwhile Piero had shown his true colours as an arrogant man with no charisma, eminently unsuited to guide the fragile Florentine 'Republic'. Alfonsina didn't get involved, turning instead to Savonarola and an initial enthusiasm for the sermons of the scourge of the Renaissance. But the events that took place after the death of the Magnifico in 1492 transformed her from an ordinary noblewoman into a leader.

Piero il Fatuo,
son of Lorenzo il Magnifico

In 1494 the French invaded Italy. Piero had been unable to stop them, despite surrendering possessions, including fortresses, to the French king Charles VIII. This was just what Savonarola had been waiting for: the populace rebelled and the servile Piero – who had become 'the Fatuous' was driven out in the second exile of the dynasty. While the Medici fled, Alfonsina remained alone in the family palazzo. For almost a year she stayed in Via Larga, the sole custodian surrounded by the family assets; in the end, she yielded and joined her husband. The Medici's attempts to return failed. In the vain hope of recovering power Piero joined forces with the French. It wasn't a good move, also because in 1503 the son of the Magnifico drowned while crossing the Garigliano river with weapons and cannon. Alfonsina was left a widow at the age of 33, with two adolescent children and an overweening ambition.

Once proclaimed head of the family, Piero's widow began to scheme. She made her base in Rome where she could rely on influential support. She succeeded in marrying Clarice to the banker Filippo Strozzi and in retrieving credit and connections in Florence. She kept her son Lorenzo on a very short leash: she was determined to make him a prince and all her hopes pivoted on him. Figures close to the Medici circles turned to her, including Niccolò Machiavelli. When the Holy League chased the French out of Italy in 1512, the Medici were allowed to return to Florence. Machiavelli wrote to Donna Alfonsina updating her on the downfall of the Gonfalonier Pier Soderini. It was Lorenzo il Magnifico's daughter-in-law who brought the Medici back to Florence, after nearly ten years of jockeying.

After returning to the palazzo the 'regent' undertook an intensive campaign of governance. Her brother-in-law Giuliano di Nemours, son of the Magnifico, was the designated heir, but he was more

Niccolò Machiavelli

30

of a poet than a politician and was frequently ill. Her son Lorenzo, who had become Captain General of the Church, was in the north fighting. Alfonsina began writing to Rome or to Milan, instigating – as Filippo Strozzi put it in a letter – "renown for the State, courage in allies and fear in enemies", and performing "an office which would be impossible for another woman and easy for very few men." In the margins of official documents, or minutes of government meetings, we can still find the wording "commissioned by the most illustrious Signora Alfonsina," or "by order of Madonna Alfonsina." It was she who ordered the enlargement of the family chapel in San Lorenzo, restored the Villa of Poggio a Caiano, bought and managed the marsh of Fucecchio, drained in a masterful reclamation operation. To give an idea of just how capable Alfonsina was, the website of the Municipality of Fucecchio still gratefully recalls that "in no period were so many hundreds of tons of eels caught as in the time of Donna Alfonsina."

The lady was particularly active with her brother-in-law Giovanni, the son of the Magnifico, who became Leo X. Alfonsina was on excellent terms with the Pontiff, and even organised the festivities to mark his first visit to Florence after the election. She urged him to appoint her son-in-law Filippo Strozzi as papal banker, but above all she pleaded for the Duchy of Urbino, a feud of the Holy See, for her son Lorenzo. Francesco Vettori records that "she tirelessly plagued the Pope to give her son a state." The Medici had taken refuge in Urbino during their exile, but gratitude was not at the top of Alfonsina's agenda. Eventually the Pope gave in, and in 1516 the Della Rovere were illegitimately ousted and Lorenzo became Duke of Urbi-

Portrait of Lorenzo de' Medici, Duke of Urbino.
Painted by Raphael

no. It was an unedifying deed, but no more so than Pope Borgia's machinations for his sons or the scheming of Ludovico il Moro for Milan. Nonetheless it was sufficient for Paolo Giovio to stigmatise the "blind ambition" of Donna Alfonsina as having caused the ruin of Italy.

In the space of three years Lorenzo lost the Duchy and his life, although not before marrying a descendant of the French sovereign, Madeleine de la Tour d'Auvergne. Naturally the ambitious match had been conceived by his mother, who launched the foreign dimension of the Medici matrimonial alliance policy. The joy was, however, short-lived; Madeleine died just a few days after the birth of Caterina (the future Queen of France), and her hus-

Lorenzo de' Medici, Duke of Urbino.
Marble by Michelangelo, Sacrestia Nuova, San Lorenzo, Florence

band followed her a week later. Was it syphilis? Was it poison? Alfonsina, her dreams shattered, and aware that the power she had amassed could not outlive its possessor, passed away herself only nine months later in February 1520. Filippo Strozzi, despite all the benefits he had reaped from his mother-in-law's stratagems during her life, penned a caustic epigraph that encapsulates the judgement of the time. "Alfonsina Orsini, whose death no-one will mourn, whose life everyone suffered, whose burial is inordinately pleasing to humanity." In actual fact, the wife of the inept Piero was probably not the wicked stepmother of the family but simply usurped male roles and prerogatives.

The "ambitious and importunate female" who wanted to play boys' games.

Caterina, the tiger of Forlì

"If I could write the story of my life, I would stun the world." An intrepid heroine, Caterina Sforza was the unexpected leading lady in a dynasty of warriors. She was the granddaughter of the most famous mercenary captain, Francesco Sforza, and the mother of the last of the great *condottieri*, Giovanni dalle Bande Nere. But it was also she who kept the Conclave of 1484 under artillery fire, who agreed to sacrifice her children rather than surrender the city of Forlì and who challenged and humiliated Cesare Borgia. A woman of arms and government, a chivalric paladin, she has taken her place in history not because she ushered in new times but because she stood out as a figure from ancient times. And also because she entrusted the young Giovanni to the care of Jacopo Salviati, thus saving him and the House of Medici.

Caterina Sforza

Caterina was the illegitimate daughter of Galeazzo Maria Sforza and Lucrezia Landriani, his official mistress and mother of four of his children. Her grandfather Francesco was the founder of dynastic power in Milan, and her uncle Ludovico (il Moro) the splendid usurper who schemed for twenty years until he could place the ducal crown upon his head. Brought up by her grandmother, Bianca Maria Visconti, from a tender age Caterina revealed her indomitable spirit. She was rebellious and argumentative and loved sword-fighting and hunting. The Sforza Valkyrie was tall, shapely and very blonde. She was painted by all the great artists, Botticelli in the lead, but also Leonardo. She was "a most cruel and spirited woman, almost a virago. Undoubtedly the foremost woman in Italy" (Venetian chronicler). At the age of eight she was part of the cortege that escorted the Duke of Milan to visit Lorenzo il Magnifico. She was enchanted by the Medici's palace without dungeons and tower. This visit to Florence made a lasting impression on her, but many years were to pass before the course of life was to bring her back to Via Larga again. So Caterina went back to Milan and submitted in silence to the marriage with Girolamo Riario – the spineless nephew of Pope Sixtus IV – who raped her to "get a taste before marriage". Caterina was 10 years old, and it was the last time that she obeyed.

Galeazzo gave Riario the Lordship of Imola, to which the city of Forlì was added as a gift from the Pope. Girolamo and Caterina became lords of the Romagna, a prized territory of passage for those travelling south. They had lands to rule over, even though they lived in Rome where Girolamo was serving as Captain General of the Church. But when his uncle the Pope died suddenly in 1484, Girolamo's fortunes turned. Rome was, as always, flung into chaos and terror and those who had been wronged sought revenge. In the general disorder a *condottiera* emerged; the pregnant Caterina didn't

Caterina Sforza, detail of Botticelli's Primavera.
Uffizi Gallery, Florence

think twice about placing herself at the head of her husband's knights and occupying Castel Sant'Angelo, where she remained for 12 days threatening the Vatican. She wanted the cardinals to meet in conclave and elect a new Pope to put an end to the disorder. When the fearful Girolamo came to an agreement with the cardinals, Caterina was forced to withdraw. But she did not forget that she knew how to wield the sword.

The couple left Rome and took refuge in Forlì, where Girolamo was assassinated in a plot hatched by local notables. The city was in revolt but Caterina locked herself up in the

Castel Sant'Angelo, Rome

fortress of Ravaldino and held firm, regardless of the fact that the besiegers had her six children in hostage. "Hang them if you will," she replied to the threat that her children would be murdered and, raising her skirt to reveal her genitals, added "here I have all that's required to make others." Caterina held fast in the fortress until the army of her uncle Sforza arrived and she regained possession of her realm. She became the regent for her eldest son Ottaviano, reviewed the tax system, reduced duties and controlled the militia. Nobody knew, but she had secretly married Giacomo Feo, brother of the castellan who had remained faithful to her. It was a mad and passionate love affair, from which a boy was born. But Giacomo soon entered into serious conflict with the Riario clan. Her children feared that she had lost her head and would also end up losing the State And so the stepfather fell victim to a conspiracy that seemed to involve everyone in

Forlì. Except, that is, cruel Caterina: the revenge of the tiger of Forlì was bloody and terrible, a blood bath in which whole families were slaughtered. In 1496 the ambassador of the Republic of Florence, Giovanni de Medici from the younger branch of the family, came into the life of a woman crazy with grief and solitude. Perhaps Giovanni reminded her of the happy grace of her visit to Florence, or perhaps he simply gave her a shoulder, and a city, to lean on. They were swiftly married, and in April 1498 Ludovico was born, named after Caterina's uncle, Duke of Milan. However, the happiness was not to last: six months later Giovanni fell ill and died, leaving her a widow for the third time. She was 36 and had eight children. The name of her last-born was changed to Giovanni, after his late father. The 'Bande Nere' came later.

Giovanni de' Medici il Popolano, Caterina's third and last husband

But Caterina had no time for tears. Cesare Borgia, son of the new Pope Alexander VI and now allied with the French, had set his sights on the Romagna. And while Imola opened the gates to him "like a whore", the Countess left her children in Florence and rushed to Forlì. Along with some volunteers she once again barricaded herself inside the fortress. She was hoping for help from her uncle Sforza (who had regained Milan) or from the Florentine Republic, but no-one raised a finger. Wearing armour and bearing a sword, Caterina personally led the defence. Cesare put a price on her head and bombarded the fortress day and night: it was a woman playing cat and mouse with him! On 12 December 1500 Cesare launched the last attack; 500 men died on the ramparts and the fortress was

Cesare Borgia, the terrible "Valentino"

taken. Caterina went on fighting until, alone and surrounded, she was forced to surrender. Borgia took her as his prisoner to Rome where she was locked up in Castel Sant'Angelo. For six months Caterina supported all sorts of maltreatment, but survived. She was released by the French and took refuge in Florence in the convent of the Murate along with the young Giovanni, dressed as a girl to escape the snares of those who wanted to steal his inheritance (and perhaps his life). She died of pneumonia at the age of 46 while she was still scheming to recover the lordship. She died mistress of her own destiny, the last great woman of the Middle Ages. Frightening at times, but never frightened. "If I could write the story of my life," she confided to a nun at the convent of the Murate shortly before she died, "I would stun the world."

MARIA, A LIFE DEVOTED TO COSIMO

She was the mother of the Duke. All the surviving portraits, commissioned by the Court in black and white, show her as a widow garbed in graceful melancholy, as though she had never been young. Her name was Maria, and although she was young once, even she doesn't

Shy and modest, her entire life devoted to her son, only
black and white portraits of her survive.
Maria Salviati and Cosimo de' Medici as a child.
Jacopo Pontormo, Walters Art Gallery, Baltimore, USA

remember it. Her mortified womb gave birth to only one child, destined to greatness. The boy grew up to reunite the divided branches of the family, to bring peace to the realm through force and to project it into the future. That precious child was Maria's mission in life.

Daughter of the banker Jacopo Salviati and Lucrezia de Medici (the Magnifico's first born), Maria Salviati was ten years old when Giovanni erupted into her life, and she fell instinctively and totally in love with him. He was the turbulent orphaned son of Caterina Sforza and Giovanni Il Popolano, of the younger branch of the Medici family. Before dying his mother Caterina had entrusted him to the care of the Salviati, who loved him like a son. "Be of good heart and good temper, and remember you are constantly in my heart," his adoptive mother Lucrezia wrote to him in 1514, and I recommend Maria, you should go to see her often." The Salviati planned this marriage for years, but they did no service to their daughter. Maria (from the Cafaggiolo branch) and Giovanni (from the Popolano) were completely opposite in temperament. She was retiring, modest and patient, while he was harsh, fierce and immoderate. Growing up in the woods, Giovanni was always on horseback, sword-fighting and hunting, getting mixed up in raids and scuffles. He was recalcitrant about the marriage, despite the fact that it was a wonderful opportunity for him: it would save him from the scheming of his relatives and establish him in the front ranks of the family. He hesitated, but in the end gave in. Maria married him under the illusion that she would be able to win over her husband's reluctance. But that didn't happen. Giovanni spent the 10 years of marriage on the battlefields, so much so that one wonders how they man-

Harsh, fierce and immoderate, he spent the ten years of marriage
moving from one battle to the next.
Portrait of Maria Salviati and Giovanni dalle Bande Nere.
Giovan Battista Naldini, Uffizi Gallery, Florence

aged to have a child. However, Cosimo arrived, his name chosen by Maria's uncle, the very Pope Leo X in whose service Giovanni was fighting, bearing the White Bands (which then became black after the Pope's death).

The birth of Cosimo didn't change much in his father's life. Maria's letters rebuke him gently. "It is four months since you left and I have yet to have a word from you . . ." He instead writes from the camp to his friend Francesco Albizzi: "Go and fetch that Greek lass that I left in Viterbo and send her to me here." Giovanni chased wars and women all his life; there was a Camilla in Rome and an Angelica in Venice. Maria continued to wait: "since your Lord left here I have written you 50 letters, and I have not had a reply to a single one." Giovanni appears to have pursued death on the battlefield, where he excelled: he was an outstanding captain with a sole purpose in life, constantly fleeing from himself. Meanwhile he continued to ask his wife for money to fund his exploits and his wom-

Portrait of Giovanni dalle Bande Nere. *Francesco da Sangallo, Bargello, Florence*

Cuirass of Giovanni
dalle Bande Nere.
Museo Stibbert, Florence

en. So much so that at one point Maria had to reprimand him. "Here we have no fodder or anything. Or wheat to eat." Giovanni replies telling her to ask her uncle, the Pope, for the money.

But there wasn't time. In 1526 the young captain of the Bande Nere was seriously wounded in the leg by the Imperial Landsknechts (heading towards Rome with Charles V) and died of gangrene. The death of this man who was never satisfied left the papal troops stunned and converted a part-time widow into a full-time one. Maria was 27 years old and, although "still fresh and good-tempered," she rejected the offers of all suitors. Just as she had lived clinging to her empty marriage, so she sacrificed herself to her only son to make him into the man he was destined to be. "As soon as the lord my consort lost his life, I decided that I would live for ever with my son, since I would be much happier staying at his side than leaving him." Maria and Cosimo lived a modest, dignified and

Maria Salviati and her son Cosimo spent many years here at the Castello del Trebbio living a modest, dignified and peaceful existence

peaceful existence at the Castle of Trebbio. Living nearby was another Maria (Soderini) and her son Lorenzino, also of the younger branch. The two boys grew up together as friends, but their destiny was to become rivals and later one was assassinated on commission from the other.

Far from the shenanigans of the Palazzo, Cosimo grew up into a strong, healthy and taciturn young man. Despite the limited resources his mother nurtured the education of this great-grandson of the Magnifico: hunting and swordsmanship, but also Latin and the classics. Maria asked Filippo Strozzi for help to pay off the debts, and in 1530 she sent her son to attend the coronation of Charles V in Bologna. Although any chance of his coming to reign seemed remote, Cosimo brought together the blood of both branches of the family and his mother wanted the emperor to know. Maria worked with insight and patience When the Cafaggiolo Medici returned to power, she managed to place young Cosimo in the retinue of Duke Alessandro, whom he accompanied on trips to Naples, Rome and Venice, becoming acquainted with all the intrigues and opportunities of politics. Maria continued to guide him in his education for princehood. In 1537 the despotic Duke Alessandro was assassinated by Lorenzino, eliminating the main branch of the family in one fell swoop. The 17-year-old Cosimo was prepared, and when he was approached for election as head of government he agreed. However those who had believed it would be easy to manipulate this modest country boy soon had to think again. In less than one year the son of Giovanni of the Bande Nere, grandson of the tiger of Forlì, dismissed the councillors and assumed absolute power. He overruled and silenced those who tried to oppose him, including Filippo Strozzi who had generously come to his aid in time of need. He also commissioned the ruthless murder of Lorenzino, ten years after the crime.

And so Maria became the mother of the Duke: her life's purpose had been accomplished, she had won the wager. She became a grandmother, taking care of Cosimo and Eleonora's many children. Contemptuous of power, she

Portrait of Cosimo de' Medici.
Alessandro Allori, Galleria Borghese, Rome

even refused the provision allocated to her and – although there was always an apartment ready in Palazzo Vecchio – she returned to Trebbio. The artificer rather than spectator of the most dazzling political career ever, Maria disappeared from the scene as silently as she had lived.

ELEONORA AT THE PALAZZO

A woman in Palazzo della Signoria? Unheard of!

When in 1540 Eleonora of Toledo, wife of Duke Cosimo I, entered the ancient seat of the republican government to transform it into a ducal residence, there were those in Florence who shook their heads. Since the time of Dante these rooms had been occupied only by the Gonfalonier and the Priors, and no woman had ever set foot inside. However the (somewhat dated) private quarters of Via Larga were no longer sufficient to hold the dreams of the family: Eleonora and Cosimo needed new spaces for their new ambitions. They wanted a court to live in and to show off. And so they moved lock, stock and barrel into Palazzo Vecchio, which they enlarged, renovated and embellished. They also filled the attics on the top floor with children. The Duchess herself took over the Gonfalonier's apartment. By installing themselves within this symbol of power, the Dukes conveyed a very clear message to their fellow citizens. There would be no more discreet exercise of personal influence; the Medici were no longer *primi inter pares*, they were first, full stop. By now their dominion was absolute.

Eleonora was a superb sovereign, chosen – like others before her – for her name. Her father, Don Pedro de Toledo, was viceroy of Naples and lieutenant of the Emperor Charles V. When she arrived in Florence, Eleonora brought with her immense riches and influential relatives, fundamental for the consolidation of the nascent Tuscan state. She also brought a marmoreal beauty: Don Pedro had decided to give Cosimo the hand of his eldest daughter, but the Duke insisted, he wanted the second-born. He had already seen her in Naples when he was very young and had remained captivated. Don Pedro agreed, and Eleonora arrived on 29 June 1538. It was a political marriage, and it became a union of interests. In addition, something which was very rare at the time, it also proved a solid sentimental alliance.

Blonde hair, blue eyes and a haughty demeanour, sumptuous and bejewelled, the Duchess travelled through the city in a velvet litter without ever showing herself, as in a tabernacle. She was accompanied by a strictly Spanish retinue, (to whom the Spanish Chapel in Santa Maria Novella was assigned), and continued to speak in Spanish. As a courtly princess destined to a palace, Florence was a little small for Eleonora. But in private the duchess was "a bird with her chicks", as her husband called her, a wise housewife, shrewd administrator and attentive to her children. Cosimo and Eleonora: a couple proof against extra-conjugal dalliance. She knew how to deal with him, how to temper his impetuosity; he respected her and was faithful. They frequently travelled together, and rode and hunted, and had an intense correspondence. In their private contracts they both expressly prohibited disposing of their assets to anyone other than consort or children. In a word, a solid matrimonial pact that built into a joint economic, political and sentimental project. Cosimo and Eleonora loved each other.

When the duke was absent, Eleonora was the Head of State, aided by the fact that she got on famously with her mother-in-law Maria Salviati. The duchess was a staunch

Cosimo I.
Bronzino, Uffizi Gallery, Florence

Catholic, and was responsible for bringing the Jesuits to Florence. She also brought extraordinary skill to bear on the management of the considerable private fortune – her own and that of her husband – especially after the war for the conquest of Siena had emptied the ducal coffers. Between one child and the next (she gave birth to 11 in all), she marketed wheat and made loans, purchased houses and farms, reclaimed marshland for agriculture and even bought Florentine public debt bonds. Even the Duke himself borrowed vast sums of money from his wife. Under Eleonora the family assets, which had been in decline for some time, began to grow again, making new expenditure possible. After ten years in the Palazzo della Signoria, the family decided that they needed more space,

Eleonora of Toledo.
In the last years of her life the duchess
appeared tired, worn out and thin.
Florentine school, copy of Bronzino, private collection, Assisi

and that the rooms of the mediaeval building had too
little light and insalubrious air. Once again it was Eleonora who paid out of her own funds the 9,000 florins to buy
the Boboli farm. At the time of purchase the building had
no roof and reached only to the first floor, but it had the
makings of a fine residence. Cosimo summoned Amman-

nati, Tribolo and Buontalenti to renovate and enlarge the building, surrounding it with gardens and citrus groves, and the family packed their bags once again. Much of the parabola of Florentine history is encapsulated in these moves (of power): from the Republic of the ashlar-clad residence of Via Larga, to the frescoed Duchy of Palazzo della Signoria, to the Grand Duchy of the courtly salons of the Pitti Palace.

From here Eleonora saw the start of building of the Uffizi, but she did not live long enough for Vasari's corridor. Bronzino portrays her tired and drawn in a portrait now in Berlin. For years she had been suffering from tuberculosis, but she suffered even more for her offspring. While she had been lucky in her marriage, she was not lucky with her children. She had already buried five of them: three while they were still infants, then her eldest daughter Maria, who died of malaria aged 17, and Lucrezia, probably mur-

Giovanni, son of Cosimo I.
Agnolo Bronzino,
Uffizi Gallery, Florence

Garcia de' Medici.
Agnolo Bronzino,
Uffizi Gallery, Florence

dered by her husband the Duke of Ferrara. But the series of deaths did not end there. In 1562 the duchess went with Cosimo to Maremma to inspect some of the forts; they were accompanied by their sons Giovanni, Garcia and Ferdinando. During a stop at the Castle of Rosignano, the three boys fell ill with malaria, and within a month first Giovanni and then Garcia died. Worn out with grief, Eleonora too died, six days after Garcia. Only Ferdinando managed to recover (and later took over from his brother Francesco as Grand Duke). However a different version of this domestic tragedy soon began to spread throughout Italy, one that has moreover recently been confirmed by the discovery in the historic archives of an official family tree commissioned by the Medici in 1712. Garcia, jealous of Giovanni, stabbed him during a hunting party, and was then mortally wounded by Cosimo who was enraged at the loss of his favourite son. Whatever version is true, one can die of grief, and that is what happened to the most powerful woman in Florence. And she still looks out at us, immortal – and perhaps a little sad – through the eyes of Bronzino in the portrait showing her with her arm around the infant Giovanni, who never grew to manhood.

Eleonora of Toledo
with her son Giovanni.
She was haughty and astute
and under her skilful
management
the family assets grew.
Agnolo Bronzino,
Uffizi Gallery, Florence

Isabella, betrayed in the family

Strangled with a rope by an Orsini, with the hand of a Medici on the noose. This is how Isabella, the third-born child of Cosimo I and Eleonora of Toledo and the most cultured, extroverted and high-spirited of the Medici princesses, met her end. Not one – not even the Medici queens who ruled in France – could rival her brilliance, enthusiasm and passionate interests. But she was assassinated by her husband, with the benevolent consent of her brother. The splendour of the dynasty went with her to the grave, and the sun set for ever on the court that had nurtured culture.

Isabella was the apple of her father's eye. She studied Greek at the age of five and by the age of nine was writing Latin verses "longer than a Bible". When she was eleven she was betrothed to Paolo Giordano Orsini, to seal the ancient bond with the powerful Roman family for the third time. It turned out a very bad deal for the Medici, and above all for the impulsive Isabella. Orsini was a dissolute man, an avid gambler described by contemporaries as uncouth and arrogant. Isabella loved beauty, wrote poetry, knew about astrology and adored chivalric romances. The marriage was consummated in 1558; Isabella was sixteen and felt as if she ruled the world.

But all too soon the grand-ducal family was plunged into bereavement and despair. In the space of a few short

Cultured, passionate and brilliant: Cosimo's daughter Isabella
was the apple of her father's eye.
Mirabello Cavalori, Kunsthistorisches Museum, Vienna

years Isabella lost her sisters Maria and Lucrezia, her
mother Eleonora and her brothers Garcia and Giovanni,
to whom she had been deeply attached. She was left the
only woman of the house; her younger brothers were
entrusted to her care and she provided the elderly Duke her
father with a strong shoulder to lean on. Cosimo was
extraordinarily fond of his lively daughter, and he allotted
her an income to ensure that she never had to leave Florence. While Paolo Giordano remained in Rome, where he
set about squandering the Medici assets, Cosimo bought

Villa Baroncelli (later known as the Villa of Poggio Imperiale) for Isabella. In salons of the Villa she held court as a patron of artists and culture, gathering the Florentine intellectuals around her. It seemed as if Isabella had inherited the ardour of her great-grandmother Caterina Sforza, revealing the same passion and daring. The meetings she organised included theatricals, the study of Aristotle and performances of the loves and follies of Ariosto's Orlando. In the years of the Counter-Reformation, Isabella's circle moved against the tide, nourishing itself on a mythological and fantastic world with at its centre a Man devoid of dogma, reared in the cult of the Greek *paideia* and driven by the search for happiness.

Isabella was tireless. After two miscarriages, she gave birth to three children: Isabella, Eleonora and Virginio. She went around the city in a carriage drawn by white horses, always packed with her intellectual friends. Her favourite companion on these jaunts was her cousin Leonora of Toledo, a Spanish noblewoman who had married her brother Pietro. Although Isabella found it impossible to see eye to eye with her brother Francesco, who had become Duke after Cosimo's abdi-

Portrait of Virginio Orsini, Duke of Bracciano, son of Isabella and Paolo Giordano Orsini.
Florentine artist,
Uffizi Gallery, Florence

Portrait of Isabella's father Cosimo I, who protected her as long as he lived.
Agnolo Bronzino,
Studiolo di Francesco,
Palazzo Vecchio, Florence

cation, she made friends with Bianca Cappello, his official mistress. Isabella displayed a lust for life that not everyone appreciated. Moreover, since her husband by now openly betrayed her with Vittoria Accoramboni, a woman of minor nobility but major ambitions, while her husband presented his mistress at court and Pietro was consistently unfaithful to Leonora, why could she too not let herself go and love (almost) secretly the cultured, polite and refined Troilo Orsini? But Isabella's feeling of omnipotence was built on sand.

As long as Cosimo lived, she and her cousin were safe. But after the old lion died in 1574 there was no one to hold the family together or curb its excesses. Francesco, now Grand Duke to all intents and purposes, forgot Isabella's help in introducing Bianca Cappello to the court. The first thing he did was to cut off his sister's income and put an end to her literary circles and other affectations. He also cancelled the bequests that his father had left to his grandchildren. Isabella protested and they argued bitterly. Francesco was a vengeful alchemist and not a forgiving man. And his brother-in-law urged him on, pointing out that Isabella was bringing disgrace on the family, while her brother said the same about Leonora. The two murders were carefully planned in advance.

Things came to a head in 1575: Orazio Pucci, with one of the Frescobaldis and a Ridolfi, hatched a plot to get rid of the Medici brothers. The conspiracy was discovered and the revenge was bloody and terrible. The twenty conspirators were hung by the neck and their goods confiscated. Leonora's name was tied up with the conspiracy, which was the opportunity Pietro had been waiting for to make room in the conjugal bed. On 10 July 1576 Leonora was strangled in the Medici villa of Cafaggiolo. She appears to have struggled desperately for her life, biting her husband so hard on the hand that he had to keep it bandaged for several weeks. Francesco personally justified the occurrence to King Philip II of Spain: "My brother Don Pietro took her life himself for having betrayed him by behaving in a manner unworthy of a noblewoman."

Isabella felt danger approaching, but it was too late. When she heard the news about Leonora, by a sad coincidence she herself was already in another of the Medici villas at Cerreto Guidi. She thought that her days were numbered, instead she only had a matter of hours. That evening the dwarf Morgante and her lady-in-waiting accompanied her to the door of her bedroom. They didn't want to leave her, but Orsini drove them away. She never left the room alive. This was just six days after the murder of Leonora. The distraught husband announced to the world that his wife had died while "washing her hair". In a sordid ostentation of power Francesco displayed his sister's tortured body "all black from the waist up, and snow-white from the waist down." The Florentine ambassador in Vienna told the Duke candidly that no-one there believed that of the two cousins "one died of apoplexy and the other of epilepsy". Bianca Cappello took Isabella's linens and also her children. A year later Troilo was killed in Paris. Following the 'mysterious' death of her husband, Orsini married Vittoria Accoramboni. Honour was saved.

THE WHITE LADY, BIANCA AT COURT

"Your Highness, where should we bury the Grand Duchess?"

"Wherever you want, but not with us."

So, we do not even know the whereabouts of the tomb of the noblewoman who was first mistress and later wife of the Grand Duke Francesco I: Bianca Cappello, the courtesan who dared to become a duchess. Possibly no other woman has been so maltreated by the Florentines – in life and in death – as this aristocratic Venetian who arrived in Florence as a fugitive and went on to become the first lady of the Tuscan court. For centuries she has been alternately scoffed at and absolved by history. Yet her life was not a soap opera, but rather a love story that lasted through the years, surviving beyond passion and despite aging, defying the intrigues, the city and the whole of Italy. It was able to survive her marriage to another man and the birth of a daughter, and his marriage to another woman (the daughter of the Emperor to boot) and the birth of eight children. It was able to withstand public scandal when he became Regent of Tuscany and then Duke, and when her husband was (providentially?) assassinated. The flaunted love affair was awkward and objectionable, like a Renaissance Prince Charles and

Camilla story, yet love all the same, with its baggage of guilt and suffering. It was sealed by a royal wedding after a life spent (almost) in secret, and was shared in death which overtook the couple just a few hours from each other. Eros and Thanatos: no fairy tale, just the earthly and sublime brutality of life.

Born into a noble Venetian family, Bianca was only eleven when her mother died. The beautiful Pellegrina Morosini left her a wealth of jewels, but also

An unbreakable bond was forged instantly between Bianca Cappello (in the portrait) and Duke Francesco
Alessandro Allori,
Palatine Gallery, Florence

condemned her to the despotic regime of a powerful and jealous stepmother, a certain Lucrezia Grimani. Bianca was intelligent and cultured, and grew up with her nose pressed against the window of the palace on the Grand Canal dreaming of escape. The dream materialised in the shape of Piero Buonaventuri, who was only a humble bank clerk but to win the lady passed himself off as the scion of a family of noble Florentine merchants. The elopement that followed – probably hastened by an unexpected pregnancy – drew down upon the couple the anger of her family, namely the Republic of Venice, and put a price on her head. This was in December 1563. The case became diplomatic and ended up in the hands of Francesco, delegated by his father to deal with the matter. And he did it so well that he lost his head. The by now legitimately married couple were not returned to Venice, but nor were they permitted to leave Florence. And while Piero suddenly found himself with money and prestigious assignments, the soft and glowing Bianca, who had become a mother in the modest Buonaventuri home, began to dream once more of escape, this time with a real prince. The bond between them was instant and enduring, and Bianca had a powerful influence over the introverted prince. Cosimo was not at all happy about it, and wrote concernedly to his son: "Going around Florence alone at night does not look good," especially because it is becoming "a habit". A habit that soon had the whole city gossiping.

However, Francesco had to fulfil his grand-ducal duties and take himself a wife to generate heirs. The choice fell on

Francesco I de' Medici.
Santi di Tito,
Uffizi Gallery, Florence

Joanna of Austria
and her son Filippo.
*Giovanni Bizzelli,
Uffizi Gallery, Florence*

the colourless Joanna of Austria, who was welcomed triumphantly in 1565. But the beautiful Venetian never left the sovereign's life; she was introduced at court, installed in a palazzo in Via Maggio and showered with gifts and properties. And things might have stayed that way: a ménage a quatre marked by clear-cut roles. Piero Buonaventuri – dubbed the 'Golden Cuckold' by his waggish fellow citizens – was busy enjoying the fruits of his wife's relationship. Meanwhile the imperial bride was neglected in everything but her husband's zeal, which caused her to give birth to no less than six princesses all in a row. "The prince loves you," her father-in-law Duke Cosimo wrote to Joanna to reassure her, inviting her to "make peace, allow his youthful age to run its course and bear prudently what time will shortly heal." And there was Bianca, all set to give Francesco the male heir that was eluding Joanna. But, as it turned out…

As it turned out, for once time gave Cosimo the lie, things went out of kilter and a series of deaths paved the way to the throne for the patient mistress. In 1572 Piero Buonaventuri was murdered, victim of one of the amorous intrigues in which he had engaged to assuage his wounded pride. It was said that Francesco knew of it and may even have been an accomplice to the crime. But was it really in the Regent's interests to cast off this last semblance of decency? Two years later, Cosimo's death swept away any of the new Duke's lingering scruples and the presence of Bianca in the public life of the city became official. Then finally two sons arrived: Antonio, born to Bianca, and Filippino (who died at the age of five) to Joanna. Shortly afterwards cruel fate also removed the sad princess from the scene when, pregnant again, she fell down the steps of the church of Santissima Annunziata. Less than two months later the most improbable outcome materialised when, in June 1578, Francesco secretly married the love of his life. Venice, after having ostracised Bianca, now opened its arms towards its "beloved daughter". But although the enemies of the Grand Duchess began to dwindle,

Don Antonio, son of Bianca and Francesco, lived constantly in the shadow of his uncle Ferdinando. He is shown here in a detail from the painting "The Marriage of Maria de Medici and Henry IV of France".
Jacopo da Empoli,
Uffizi Gallery, Florence

Florence refused to pardon the long affair and invented a mocking ditty along the lines of: "The Tuscan Grand Duke has married a whore,/ Who was a Venetian noble before." Nevertheless, Bianca was satisfied with her restored respectability and behaved impeccably; she was generous with her husband's daughters and affable with her forbidding brother-in-law Ferdinando. She had no political ambitions and did not scheme. Her sole torment was that she could not conceive another child. The only outcome of all the medicines, diets and magic potions and the frenzied conjugal embraces was a false pregnancy. Bianca preferred the peace of the Villa of Pratolino to the bustle of court life but it was at a hunting party in another Medici Villa, at Poggio a Caiano, that she and her husband met their fate.

Ferdinando I.
Scipione Pulzone,
Uffizi Gallery, Florence

On 19 October 1587, after days of identical symptoms and atrocious pain, they passed away just 11 hours from one another. It was all too easy to point the finger at the fortunate beneficiary of the tragedy, Cardinal Ferdinando, who did not even wait for the duchess to die before rushing to Florence to ensure his immediate succession.

Even the Pope, when he learnt that the Duke's brother had been in the villa at the time, let slip that "the world will have a lot to say about that." However, recent analyses appear to rule out the theory of poisoning, having found evidence of malarial fever. What does seem certain on the other hand – at least to some historians – is that it was only after the death of the couple that various papers, testimony and confessions came to light accusing Bianca of having falsely claimed Antonio as her son when he was actually the child of a servant. The boy was thus transformed overnight from a potential heir to an intruder, although strangely enough – and through the good offices of Ferdinando – he was assigned an adequate life annuity and went on to become a Knight of Malta. Ferdinando was apparently storing up all his contempt to heap it on the memory of his sister-in-law. He ordered everything that had belonged to her to be destroyed: furnishings, coats of arms, letters and works of art. The same held for her body, whose final resting-place is unknown. Even the Villa of Pratolino fell into disuse. *Damnatio memoriae*. Bianca was to exist no longer; perhaps she never had.

Caterina, the Iron Lady

A tyrant with a lust for power or an astute diplomat? An unscrupulous adventuress or a tireless mediator? And why not a mother striving to defend the rights of her children, born to her when she had resigned herself to being sterile? For ten years Caterina de Medici tried in vain to provide her consort, Henry II of France, with an heir. For ten years her greatest ally was none other than her husband's official mistress, Diane de Poitiers. When, in 1544, a child was finally brought into the world, both women heaved a sigh of relief. The throne was safe, repudiation avoided, along with the threat of a new, more beautiful and seductive (and above all, less tolerant) queen. Caterina was thus able to devote herself serenely to a close succession of pregnancies and births. Henry II, on the other hand, remained true to the icy Diane, humiliating Caterina and forcing her to live in the shadows. She was left to seek allies in the superb Valois court and manoeuvre her way through the intrigues, and also to latch onto Nostradamus and his prophecies. When the King died in 1559 the Florentine Cinderella was forced to make a decision: to come out into the open and take the reins of power into her hands. After 27 years of silent submission, the foreign bride who had been imposed by the Pope, the noblewoman of minor rank who had never gone down well at the

French court, became Queen. Rather, she became the Black Queen, destined to leave her mark.

She wasn't beautiful, she had the protruding Medici eyes and her features were not delicate. But she never lacked ingenuity, amiability and tenacity, and she had an iron will. Caterina was born in 1519, the same year as the future Duke, Cosimo. She was the last-born of the Cafaggiolo branch of the family and he of the Popolano branch. But within a few weeks the infant Caterina was orphaned of both parents, Lorenzo Duke of Urbino and Madeleine de la Tour d'Auvergne: a cradle between two coffins. And so the child was entrusted first to her grandmother, Alfonsina Orsini, and then to her aunt Clarice de Medici – the wife of Filippo Strozzi – and grew up under the wing of two successive family Popes, Leo X and Clement VII. These were carefree years, and Caterina played with her beloved Strozzi cousins. The Little duchess of Urbino (as she was called although the Duchy had already been returned to its owner) was not a beauty but shone nevertheless. She was the last legiti-

Caterina de' Medici.
Italian school,
Uffizi Gallery, Florence

mate light of the family, albeit female, the surviving symbol of the supremacy of a dynasty with a surplus of bastard heirs, from her stepbrother Alessandro to her cousin Ippolito. But she was still a good matrimonial pawn to be played on the intricate European chessboard. To keep her safe from the threats looming over Rome (such as the Sack of 1527), Caterina was sent to Florence, first to Via Larga where she came to love Ippolito and detest Alessandro, and then to Poggio a Caiano, where she was taken hostage by the republican militia. Despite the appeal of Pope Clement, the republicans held firm and the dispute continued, while the ten-year-old Caterina was moved from Via Larga to the convent of Santa Lucia and then that of the Murate, which she left on horseback with her hair cropped and dressed as a nun. These were the months of the terrible siege of 1529 by the Emperor Charles V and, above all, Pope Clement VII who wanted to reinstate the Medici and abolish the city institutions. The longer the siege dragged on the more hatred for the Medici increased, crystallising on Caterina. Florence put up a strenuous defence, despite starvation, but finally had to surrender. The tormented little duchess survived with her spirit newly forged. The scar of this civil war never left her, making her into a paladin of peace at all costs.

When the Medici were restored under the detested Alessandro, Caterina found herself saddled with the interests of the Papacy and the ambition of the family. Her marriage was an integral part of the manoeuvres for dominion over Italy between Austria and France, the Habsburgs and the Valois. The King of France, Francis I, came out on top and proposed marriage with his second son Henry, Duke of Orléans. Pope Clement was exultant. He was still smarting from the Sack of Rome by the Emperor's troops, and the

At the age of 14 Caterina was married to the son of the French king
by her uncle, Pope Clement VII. Here she is shown in the painting
"The Marriage of Caterina de Medici and Henry II".
Jacopo da Empoli, Uffizi Gallery, Florence

alliance with France seemed to offer a guarantee. In 1533,
Caterina aged 14 and married to a moody adolescent of the
same age, left for France. She brought with her the fork
(apparently the French still ate with their hands), a distillate
made for her by the friars of Santa Maria Novella (now
known as eau de cologne) and introduced the wearing of

drawers (terribly useful, especially if you like horse-riding).
Just a few years later, the sudden death of the eldest Valois
made Henry the Dauphin, after which he became King in
1547. But when Henry was accidentally and mortally
wounded in a tournament, it was Caterina who became
regent. For the next 30 years, as her four physically frail or
mentally unstable sons succeeded each other on the throne,
she was the only real monarch of France.

Caterina's main objective was to maintain the balance in
a country riven by the conflict between Catholics and Protestants, and to sustain the Crown by curbing the avidity of
the parties, keeping united a family split by ambition. But
preserving peace at all costs meant that toleration became
fluctuation, and compromise spelled uncertainty. Caterina
yielded something to one side and then something to the
other: an edict favourable to the Huguenots and a daughter
wedded to a Catholic king. This involved extenuating travels
over the length and breadth of the coun-   try to
relaunch impossible negotiations.
Not wishing to take sides, the
Queen mother ended up making
everyone discontented, exacer-
bating the intolerance of the
Catholics and the intransigence
of the Protestants. Blame for
the St. Bartholomew's Day
massacre, a political operation
that got out of hand in which
thousands of Huguenots were

Caterina, the sad princess,
a detail from the marriage painting.

72

killed, was laid entirely at her door. This led to the legend of the Black Queen, the shrewd and crafty Italian adventuress, the disciple of Machiavelli and follower of Nostradamus, who was happy to wade through blood to preserve her son's throne and her own power.

Caterina died in January 1589, faced by the failure of everything she had struggled for. Before her on her deathbed was the prospect of another civil war, and the end of the Valois dynasty. It was only in the hands of a

Portrait of Caterina de Medici, Queen of France.
Workshop of Francois Clouet, Palatine Gallery, Florence

Protestant prince – the Henry of Navarre of "Paris is well worth a mass" fame – that the Queen's ideals were gradually and fully accomplished. He achieved what she had always wanted: freedom of worship and religious tolerance. And at Henry's side was another Medici queen, Maria.

Nostradamus

73

Maria, the forgotten Queen

Maria who? The "fat banker's daughter"? There appears to be a curious consensus of judgement about the second Medici queen to arrive on the French throne. Italian historians consider her to have been haughty and presumptuous with little political acumen, their French colleagues as superficial, rather dim and irascible, while the French people saw her as a fool. A sovereign denied any tribute from posterity and, like all those who lose the game to history, she ended up carrying the can for everyone. It's true that Maria, the second of the Florentine merchant family to win the hand of a French sovereign, was not brilliant. She surrounded herself with roguish counsellors who then manipulated her, and succeeded in marginalising and eventually alienating even her son, Louis XIII. She alternated shows of pride with sudden, not very regal, psychological breakdowns, and lacked the ingenuity and dignity of the trail-blazing Caterina. But, to be fair, it was no easy task to keep afloat a throne surrounded by angry enemies. The French court of the seventeenth century was literally a nest of vipers. Maria definitely lacked skill in government, but she also had to deal with a tangle of mortal intrigues. And, more than anyone else, she was always hopelessly alone.

When her mother brought her into the world, Maria was the sixth female that her father, Francesco I de Medici, held in his arms. This was 1573, and her arrival was greeted with a sigh of disappointment; the eagerly-awaited heir was yet to come. Less than five years later the child lost her mother when the severe Duchess Joanna, daughter and grand-daughter of emperors, a humiliated princess who had never managed to integrate in Florence, died in childbirth after a nasty fall. Maria was always being left alone. Of her five older sisters, four died in infancy or shortly afterwards, and the fifth soon left Florence as the bride of the Duke of Man-tua. Even the longed-for heir Filippo, who finally arrived at the seventh attempt, did not live to the age of six. Maria also had to attend her father's marriage with Bianca Cappello, the intruder, her mother's rival. The clash was inevitable and weighed heavily on the chubby shoulders of a child who was marginalised within herself as well as at court. To fight the isolation, Maria came to rely on the daughter of the nurse, Leonora Galigai, a maid destined to play a dubious role in her life. When in 1587 Duke Francesco and his wife Bianca failed to return from the hunting party at Poggio a Caiano, having died from either poison or malaria, for a moment the 14-year-old Maria thought that she had become impor-tant. Her uncle Ferdinando switched his cassock for ermine and immediately set about banning the name of Bianca Cappello and reinstating the image of his sister-in-law Joan-na as the legitimate and late-lamented Duchess of Florence. Maria embraced life at court, preparing herself imperiously for the only role that her uncle had in mind for her from the start: a top-notch matrimonial pawn.

By the end of the sixteenth century, between loans and interest France owed the Medici almost two million *scudi*, which was a powerful reason for looking to Florence for the choice of a new candidate for queen. Henry IV of Navarre

Even at her wedding she is alone: Maria de' Medici in the painting
"The Marriage by proxy of Maria de' Medici and Henry IV".
Pieter Paul Rubens, Musée du Louvre, Paris

wanted to repudiate Margaret of Valois, known as Margot, the daughter of Caterina de Medici who had somewhat accidentally ended up reigning over France. The King was looking for a replacement capable of providing him with an heir. He may indeed have wanted to marry his latest mistress, Henriette d'Entragues, who had just borne him a son. But the debt due to Ferdinando of Tuscany weighed more in the balance than the sovereign's compulsive libido. Maria prepared herself and got married, alone as she had always been.

The magnificent wedding ceremony organised in Florence was in fact not attended by the groom, but by his representative. It was followed by a sumptuous banquet organised by Buontalenti, while Giambologna modelled statues in sugar to adorn the tables. This was the triumph of the dynasty of former merchants, the sensational culmination of a strategy that started with the Tornabuoni, continued with the Orsini and finally garnered the Houses of Toledo, Habsburg and Valois, and now that of Bourbon. Lorenzo il Magnifico would have been proud; Cosimo il Vecchio might perhaps have shuddered. Accompanying her to her departure for Marseilles, and handing over a fabulous dowry, Ferdinando gave his niece a simple but effective piece of advice: "Get pregnant!" Maria obeyed, and in ten years gave the King six children. But it was not enough; how could she compete with the nine illegitimate children born to his various mistresses over more or less the same period and recognised by the King? Henry wanted to raise them all together, but Maria objected. Even in her marriage, crowded with children but low on love, the Queen remained alone. Before Henriette she felt as Caterina had before Diane de Poitiers: besieged.

Portrait of Maria de Medici as the bride of the King of France.
Santi di Tito, Pitti Palace, Florence

She indulged in luxury, spending a fortune. She became dominated by her lady-in-waiting Galigai who, in league with her unscrupulous husband Concino Concini, took advantage of the Queen's insecurity to obtain titles and assets at the expense of the French aristocracy. When Henry was killed by a fanatic, Maria became regent on behalf of the nine-year-old Louis, although she had absolutely no idea about how to govern. Her weak authority could not withstand the rebellion of the aristocrats. While the Concinis lorded it over all, the Queen overturned her husband's policy and threw herself upon the ancient Catholic alliance between France and Spain. But her greatest mistake was to lose contact with her son Louis, whom she loved but underestimated. She humiliated and controlled him until she drove him to open conflict. Louis divested her twice, forcing her to withdraw. Maria

Maria de' Medici.
Jacopo Ligozzi, Uffizi Gallery, Florence

returned to the fray, organising plots with her other son Gastone and with the support of the rising star of Richelieu, who then betrayed her brutally by siding with Louis. The game was over, and to avoid civil war the Queen was exiled. She died in poverty in Cologne, abandoned by everyone. It seems that the only person to welcome her was Rubens. In happier times the artist had celebrated her life in 22 enormous allegorical paintings – now in the Louvre – illustrating the Queen's joyous birth, her splendid wedding, the peace of the Regency: in a word, the life she thought she'd had.

FIFTY YEARS WITH CHRISTINE

She reigned for over fifty years, longer than Queen Elizabeth of England. Christine of Lorraine ruled the destiny of the Tuscan State, for better or for worse, first as Grand Duchess, then as tutor to her son Cosimo II and finally as regent for her grandson Ferdinando II. The final analysis of this life spent on the throne is nevertheless far from positive. When Christine died, the Medici banks had barred their doors, the clergy had their fingers in all manner of pies and trade was stagnant. For Florence it was the beginning of the decline.

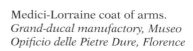

Yet Christine and her husband also lived through the last great season of Medici splendour. She was the pearl cultivated by her grandmother, the Queen of France Caterina dei Medici, to be given as a bride to the French-speaking Duke of Tuscany Ferdinando, who after the sudden death of his brother

Medici-Lorraine coat of arms.
Grand-ducal manufactory, Museo Opificio delle Pietre Dure, Florence

Portrait of Ferdinando I.
Scipione Pulzone, Medici Villa of Petraia, Florence

had doffed his cardinal's robes to take up the sceptre. It was 1587, and with this union Tuscany took a different tack in its coalition policy. No more Habsburg and Spanish brides, Ferdinando looked to Paris as the new ally to strengthen his government. Unlike his father and brother, he was convinced that only a strong France could guarantee the independence of the Italian states. And so he made direct contact with the Queen mother, who had been dispatched to France fifty years earlier by Pope Clement VII to marry the King's son, the future Henry II. Caterina, the last descendant of the ancient Cafaggiolo branch of the family, had never forgotten her homeland, and was more than happy to hand over her favourite granddaughter to the heir of the new stock initiated by Cosimo I. The princess, who was "fair-skinned, of medium height with a longish face," had three failed marriage projects behind her and a dowry of 300,000 *scudi* provided by her grandmother, concerned about her no longer tender years. Christine was in fact 22

After three failed marriage projects, Christina was married to Ferdinando de Medici.
Portrait of Christina of Lorraine.
Scipione Pulzone, Uffizi Gallery, Florence

years old and this was all to the good, as the marriage was not plain sailing, especially since the groom was already 40 and set in his egoistic ways. But she had been reared by Caterina in a good school and had acquired judgement, so that with dissimulation and patience she managed to gradually win Ferdinando over. In a word, the bride had taken her grandmother's advice to heart and in Florence she succeeded in gaining her husband's trust and the respect of the Florentines. After Joanna's aloofness and Bianca's vanity the city needed a duchess it could love. The wedding celebrations were sumptuous, rather excessively so for a former cardinal.

Ferdinando & Christine like Cosimo & Eleonora, among the few well-matched couples in the Medici family album. They had eight children and their bond was reinforced by shared intentions: simplicity in private life and magnificence in outward show. Together they restored decorum to the tumultuous court life bequeathed by Francesco I and Bianca Cappello. Ferdinando was a prince, merchant and banker, the last of the great Medici. Just as Cosimo il Vecchio and Cosimo I had done, the new Duke stimulated economic and political dynamics, fostering commerce and trade and granting mercantile concessions. He made Livorno into a free port, opening it up to Jews and Huguenots; in Pisa he built the Naviglio canal and the aqueduct, and from Arezzo presided over the reclamation of the Val di Chiana. He was also a tireless patron of the arts in Florence: he completed the Tribuna in the Uffizi, where he also housed the Medici collections in the Galleria delle Statue; he commissioned the Forte Belvedere from Buontalenti and fountains and equestrian statues from Tacca and Giambologna. Work was finally begun on the Cappella dei Principi in San Lorenzo and the Opificio delle Pietre Dure was founded. Christine too did her best; she had a passion for founding convents but was also generous to the people. Rather than shining with her own light, the Grand Duchess reflected that of an illuminated policy. She was always at her husband's side, attentive, dignified and regal. She sustained him to the core. Her frequent letters always ended with the same words "I kiss your hands with my heart." When Ferdinando died prematurely in 1609, Christine fell apart. The equilibrium in which she had lived was broken and she was unprepared to walk alone.

Heraldic emblem of Ferdinando I. Pietro Tacca, equestrian monument in Piazza Santissima Annunziata, Florence

Inexperienced and insecure, the Duchess concealed her unforeseen fragility behind a shield of hauteur. She had never been interested in governing, but now she insisted on doing it. In the effort to assert herself, her habitual religious sense became bigotry, her beliefs superstitions and relics amulets. She no longer went to mass every day, but three times a day.

Cosimo II, Maria Maddalena of Austria and their son Ferdinando.
Justus Sustermans, Uffizi Gallery, Florence

Appointed in her husband's will as tutor of their son Cosimo, Christine made a big mistake. She convinced the newly-crowned Duke that trade was unbecoming to a prince and that it was better to devote himself to study and science. This led to the closure of the Medici banks, which for years had been the primary source of the family's wealth. Furthermore, weakness made the Duchess easy prey for the ecclesiastics she had always favoured. Many of the affairs of state fell into the hands of an insolent and oppressive clergy, whose interference was not restricted to the educational system but also extended to the administration. Then there was the clash between Christine and her daughter-in-law: the Emperor's sister, Maria Maddalena of Austria, chosen by Ferdinando before his death as the wife of their son. This decision to point the needle of the scales back to Vienna again was curious, and of enormous consequence for Tuscany. So, there were two first ladies of Florence, two policies and two approaches to (mis)government: the French one embodied in Christine, and the Austrian one of the frail young Duke's wife. Rather than governing Tuscany, Cosimo himself remained holed up in the Pitti Palace. Then in 1631, at the age of just 31, he died, leaving his eleven-year-old son Ferdinando II in the hands of the two rivals, now respectively grandmother and mother. The fierce struggle continued and Tuscany was paralysed by an irresponsible matriarchate nurtured on prayers and oppression. The regents appeared to be agreed on only one thing: the exaggerated luxury of court life which made the depleted coffers of the state shudder. Christine survived Maria Maddalena too, and narrowly escaped the shame of being driven out by her grandson Ferdinando, who had finally decided to free himself of his grandmother's authority, but not that of having abandoned Galileo Galilei to his fate. It was 1633 and the Inquisition reigned supreme, while the Grand Duchy collapsed.

Portrait of Galileo Galilei.
Justus Sustermans, Palatine Gallery, Florence

Anna Maria Luisa,
the mother of the Uffizi

It's thanks to her that we have Botticelli's *Venus*, and if we have custody of Michelangelo's *Day* and *Night* or Donatello's *David*, it is due to her acumen. If every day millions of tourists crowd into the Uffizi or the Pitti Palace it is because she – Anna Maria Luisa, the last of the Medici – being unable to have a child instead brought to birth a vision: that none of the family treasures "shall ever be transferred out of the Capital". All the paintings and statues, libraries and jewels of a dynasty by now extinct were to remain in the city "for the ornament of the State, for the use of the Public and to attract the curiosity of Foreigners."

It was Maria Luisa who ensured that the city of Florence would remain a gem in the world. Being unable to take over the helm of the Duchy from her wretched brothers, or even to restore it to a civic republic, she contracted with the new sovereigns the singular legal agreement known as the 'Family Pact' destined to (re)place the Medici treasure in the hands of the city. The agreement was the brainchild of this strong-willed princess, a worthy descendant of her forbears, and she negotiated it and carried it through in the teeth of diplomatic difficulties. Forty years before Peter Leopold, it was Maria Luisa de Medici who placed the common good at the hub of political action.

per l'avvantaggio della Toscana, le A.A. LL. Reale, ed
Elettorale hanno stimato il più convenevole di regolar-
le con un Trattato, o Convenzione di Famiglia, ed hanno
autorizzato i Loro Ministri respettivi, che in virtù delle
Loro Plenipotenze comunicate da una parte, e dall'altra
sono convenuti di quel che segue.

Articolo I.

Con tutto che in conseguenza de i Trattati di Allodiali
nel Gran Ducato di Toscana sian già assicurati a S.A.R.
a titolo d'Indennità degli Allodiali che sono stati ne i
Ducati di Lorena, e di Bar, S.A. Elettorale Vedova Pa-
latina, volendo non di meno concorrere a tutte le misure
prese per il più grande Stabilimento della Tranquillità
Pubblica, e Levare sino il minimo pretesto che potesse essere
allegato un giorno a suo pregiudizio, rimette, cede, e tra-
sferisce a S.A.R. tutti i Dritti, e Pretensioni qualunque, e per qualunque titolo, o causa si sia, che Ella
potesse avervi.

Articolo II.

La Ser.ma Elettrice assicura al presente a S.A.R. per lui,
e suoi Successori, come Gran Duca di Toscana, tutti
gli Allodiali situati fuori della Toscana, tanto quelli
che le possano appartenere della Successione del Ser.mo Gran
Duca suo Fratello, che quelli, che provengono, e le appar-
tengono della Successione delle Serenissime Gran Duchesse
Sua Madre, ed Ava, per averne La proprietà, ed il
godimento alla Morte di S.A. Elettorale.

Italian translation of the Family Pact signed in Vienna in 1737.
State Archives, Florence

She was born in 1667, beautiful and spirited. Her mother, the capricious Marguerite Louise d'Orléans, should never have left France. She hated the man destiny fated her to marry and the children she bore him and the 'miserable' city she was cooped up in. And so she returned to France, and it was her grandmother, Vittoria della Rovere, who reared the child who "got prettier with every year that passed". Maria Luisa was the favourite of her father, Cosimo III. She was intelligent and lively, rode like a

Anna Maria Luisa de' Medici as a young girl.
Anton Domenico Gabbiani, Medici Treasury, Pitti Palace, Florence

man, went hunting and shooting. But she also loved music, knew Latin, and absorbed the beauty that surrounded her. There were long negotiations about her marriage, first with the King of Portugal and later with the Dauphin of Louis XIV. But the family strongboxes were empty and the dowry was meagre. The alliance waltz shifted in the direction of Austria, and it was the Emperor himself who put forward the name of the Empress's brother, Johann Wilhelm of Saxony, Elector Palatine of the Rhine. Johann was not handsome, but he was a cultured man and, above all, exuded a smiling serenity that gave Maria Luisa a peace she had never known. In 1691, in her letters from Düsseldorf, she declared herself "the happiest bride in the

Anna Maria Luisa and Johann Wilhelm, a close-knit couple.
Portrait of the Electors dancing.
Jan Frans van Douven, Palatine Gallery, Florence

world." Despite this, she was a little homesick: "I have been to Cologne," she wrote, "but to find such cities beautiful you would have to not have been born in Florence." Nevertheless, in the icy German palaces she found release from the intrigues of court, from her mother's folly and her father's depression, her grandmother's tears, her brothers' scandals and the ever-present threat of the extinction of the dynasty: "Here we are very quiet and united, and the Elector's affection for me grows by the day." Maria Luisa and Johann had a harmonious marriage. She gave impetus to the family collecting and he became an attentive patron of the arts. Many pleasant years passed at the court, amidst music and sleigh rises, hunting and balls. The only shadow was that of sterility. The Electress tried everything, even the thermal baths at Aquisgrana, but to no avail. Neither she, nor her brothers Ferdinando and Gian Gastone in Florence, succeeded in generating an heir. Even Cosimo's last desperate attempt – getting his younger brother to throw off his cardinal's hat and marry the young Eleonora Gonzaga – came to nothing, since the eagerly-awaited cousin failed to be born. The dynasty was condemned.

When the Elector Palatine died of a heart condition, in 1716 Maria Luisa decided to return home to take her place beside her father, who had already lost his elder son and his brother. She returned to embrace Florence, and for several years attempted to bind the Florentine nobility to the family, as well as becoming a regulator of the Council. It was a political role, and perhaps a last attempt at a de facto legitimisation of her candidacy to guide the Duchy. But to no avail: no European sovereign ever took seriously the idea that the (sterile) daughter of the Grand Duke could reign. When Cosimo died, the depraved Gian Gastone ascended the throne, and while Maria Luisa was relegated to Villa La Quiete it was the wars and peace treaties played out over the continent to decide the fate of Tuscany. Austrians or Spaniards? The Grand Duchy was promised to Don Carlos, but in the end Austria got the upper hand and the Florentines became citizens of the Holy Roman Empire again. In July 1737, Gian Gastone had not been dead two weeks before the Medici insignia were taken down from the door of Palazzo Vecchio and replaced by those of Franz Stephan of Lorraine. From then on the orders came from Vienna.

Tired and ill, Maria Luisa returned to the Pitti Palace where she confined herself in one wing. And while friends and advisers prostrated themselves before the new Lord of Florence – represented by the viceroy, the Prince of Craon and his clique – the Electress

Florence owes everything to her. Anna Maria Luisa de Medici, Electress Palatine. *Alfonso Boninsegni, cast in bronze in 2004 from the 1946 model, Medici Chapels, San Lorenzo, Florence* found the strength to invent the deed that was to make her mark in history. The Lorraine dynasty were only to "conserve", and could not deprive the city of its treasures, its paintings, statues, cameos, books, Etruscan and Egyptian antiquities, porcelain and tapestries. This was the gift the last of the Medici made to the city, continuing up to her death with the reorganisation of the art collections. With her, the family book was closed: after 300 years in power the Medici became extinct. "Give me any ordinary man and with a few metres of red cloth I shall make him a gentleman," Cosimo il Vecchio had said. It was a dynasty of merchants turned bankers and converted to princes, art patrons for their own pleasure rather than the public good. But these merchants in their red cloaks changed the course of history, nurturing trade and intrigues, stimulating prosperity and fierce opposition. They funded the Renaissance, built a Kingdom and hurled Tuscany into the firmament of European states. But the ancient ingenuity of the more far-sighted had deteriorated into the vacuous bigotry of the last generations. Maria Luisa's gesture was, in a way, an attempt to balance the books. The Electress died of a tumour in February 1743. It was Carnival and the Florentines accompanied her to her last repose complaining because the carnival parade had been cancelled for the funeral procession. That's Florence for you.

Printed in Florence
by Polistampa Firenze srl
July 2023